Look a Gorilla in the Eye

What Country Am I?

MC PAQUIN

ISBN: 1927833590
ISBN-13: 9781927833599

CONTENTS

ACKNOWLEDGEMENT

(: TERRY :)

Note on the Format

The "What Country Am I?" series of books provides a fun way to learn geography. Each book gives personal and fun hints about 10 countries. After the hints for each country are given, the reader is asked, *"What country am I?"* To give a true taste of each country, the hints focus on people and human interest stories.

The "What Country Am I?" series of books was written by MC Paquin, a teacher who wanted to make geography fun for her students.

1   Man-Eating Lions

What country would you be visiting if you saw a security guard who belonged to the Masai tribe?

Here are some more hints.

1. I'm a country on the continent of Africa. English is my official language because Britain ruled me for 75 years.

2. The baboons in my country love to play tricks on people. If you plant rice seedlings on a mudflat, they might wait until you leave and then pull out all the seedlings.

3. In 1898, when a railway was being built in my country, lions killed and ate many railway workers. Some lions became so bold that they even went inside tents to get their victims. The lions would grab the men by the throat and drag them off to eat them. The railway workers were terrified. They dug holes in the ground to sleep in at night so that the lions couldn't get them.

On one section of the railway, there were two terrifying man-eating lions. The railway workers were scared out of their wits and refused to work until the lions were killed. It took a hunter three weeks to lure and shoot the two lions from a hide-away in a tree.

4. There's a group of people in my country called the Masai. They are wandering cattle herders who are great warriors. Some of them now live in cities. Business people like to hire them as security guards.

5. My capital city is Nairobi. It has many tall buildings. If you look out the windows of one of these buildings, you can see far off into the distance to the plains, where giraffes, zebras, and antelope still roam.

6. When you think of me, think of big game reserves, coffee plantations, and scenery that is out of this world.

7. My people have names like Jomo Kenyatta, Aluna Mboya, and Oginga Odinga.

8. One of my mountains is Mount Kenya. This is a big hint about my name.

What country am I?

Answer: Kenya.

Point of Interest:

People from around the world like to come to my country to go on a wildlife seeing safari.

The first day of your safari, you will leave early in the morning to get to your base in the wilderness, which is often more glamorous than the best hotels in the world. Many safari tours have luxury tents with plenty of hot water for bucket showers, and the food is wonderful.

During your stay, you will be driven through the savanna. Prepare to be excited because you will see many amazing animals: not only the big five, which are the lion, elephant, Cape buffalo, leopard and rhinoceros, but also wildebeests, antelope, zebras, and cheetahs. And the tour guides are amazing. They understand the animal movements so well that they can tell by the movements of the antelope if lions are nearby. Some guides are Masai warriors.

2 All Those Islands!

What country would you be visiting if you saw a mountain where 1500 monks live?

Here are some more hints.

1. I'm in Europe.

2. When you think of me, think "All those islands!" As well as a mainland, I have 1400 islands. That's why tourism is so huge in my country. People from all over the world visit me to enjoy my blue skies, sandy beaches, and blue water.

3. On the mainland, I have a mountain called Mount Athos, which is home to 1500 monks. Women haven't been allowed to visit Mount Athos for 1000 years.

4. My people love hanging out at coffee bars. They sit outdoors on old wooden chairs at small round tables. When you visit me, why not do as they do? Relax, drink a cup of coffee, people-watch, and gossip. Be warned: our coffee is dark, thick, and very strong.

5. I was famous in ancient times for the Oracle of Delphi, an important shrine where there was a fortune teller: the priestess of the god Apollo. She communicated with the gods in order to see into the future.

One day in 548 BC, Croesus, who was King of Lydia and one of the richest men in the world, sent a messenger to the town of Delphi to ask the priestess if he should invade the Persian Empire. The priestess answered, "If King Croesus attacks the Persians, he'll destroy a mighty empire." Greatly encouraged, Croesus invaded the Persian Empire, and the priestess' prediction came true, a mighty empire was destroyed: Croesus' empire.

6. When you think of me, think of donairs, ouzo, feta cheese, olives, and Socrates.

7. My people have names like Demetrius Dimitrios, Athena Kapetanakis, and Stavros Andropoulos.

8. In my capital city, Athens, you'll see ruins of 2500-year-old temples next door to modern buildings.

What country am I?

Answer: Greece.

Points of Interest:

Croesus' name is still used today in a saying. If a person is incredibly rich, another person might say that he or she is "as rich as Croesus!"

The priestess of Apollo often gave answers that had double meanings or that weren't clear. This meant that she could never be proven wrong.

For a very relaxing time, people often vacation a couple of weeks on my island of Crete, where there's a lot of nice beaches and a lot of water to swim in.

3 The Desert Patrol

What country would you be visiting if you saw a desert patrol officer on a camel?

Here are some more hints.

1. I'm in the Middle East. My official language is Arabic.

2. Eighty percent of my land is desert, where you may see a small patch of greenery: an oasis. The presence of an oasis means there's water nearby.

3. The Dead Sea is found on my border. It's a large body of water with huge, bizarre crystal formations sticking out from the surface. The Dead Sea is so salty that it's impossible for you to sink in it. If you run into the water, your feet will be forced up from under you and you'll float so high that swimming will be impossible. Be warned: close your mouth tightly. The sea water tastes awful. Almost no living thing can live in the Dead Sea because it's so salty: that's why it's called the Dead Sea.

4. Most of my people are Muslim. Many women wear head scarves and full-length, long-sleeved dresses, but these tend to be modern, and most women aren't veiled. Many of my people wear Western fashions.

5. Women's rights improved a lot with King Hussein. He was a kind ruler who encouraged the education of women. He said, "It is my belief that to not educate women is to lose out on half of the national treasure."

6. My people have names like Muhammad Hassan, Abdullah Qazi, and Hessa Begim.

7. The Jordan River is on my western border. This is a big hint about my name.

8. For many years, I was called Transjordan, but now my name is shorter.

What country am I?

Answer: Jordan.

Points of Interest:

If you visit me, you'll be treated with Arab hospitality and kindness, but dress modestly to avoid irritating my people: men can wear shorts, but women should wear pants or a skirt that goes down at least as far as the knees, and their shoulders should be kept covered.

My capital city, Amman, is one of the leading centers of finance and trade in the Middle East.

4 Look a Gorilla in the Eye

What country would you be visiting if you saw people eating rolexes?

Here are some more hints.

1. I'm a country on the continent of Africa. Many of my people speak Swahili. One of my official languages is English because Britain ruled me for over 50 years.

2. In my capital city, Kampala, people don't wear rolexes, they eat them! A rolex is a freshly cooked chapatti, which is like a thin pancake, wrapped around an omelette, chopped onions, tomatoes, green peppers and thinly sliced cabbage. You can buy rolexes from street vendors.

3. I'm one of the few countries where you can see gorillas in the wild. When these gentle giants see you, they'll stop what they're doing, such as eating a piece of bamboo, to look at you. When their thoughtful eyes meet yours, you'll be shocked by how human they seem. But be careful: don't photograph gorillas using a flash. Flashes annoy them and they may charge you, grab your camera, rough you up, and sit on you. Since male gorillas can be three times as big as a man, you could easily get damaged.

4. If you like adventure, I'm the perfect holiday destination. Visit me, and you can white-water raft the rapids on the Nile River, cruise the Kazinga Channel where elephants drink from the nearby shore, hike into rainforests where you might see chimpanzees, bungee jump from a cliff, or watch crocodiles lurking on the sandbanks of the Nile.

5. My people are friendly and welcome tourists. They have names like Kato, Mwaka, and Masani.

6. I was home to the earliest humans. In the Swahili language, the name of my country means "land of the native people". "U" in Swahili means "land", and "ganda" means "native people."

What country am I?

Answer: Uganda.

Points of Interest:

Why not visit me and stay at one of the lodges near the Murchison Falls National Park.

You can ride on old-fashioned ferries across the Nile River and see the most amazing scenery, or you can take a boat right up to the base of the spectacular Murchison Falls.

If you like animals, go on a safari tour to see the native animals, or you can visit the Ziwa Rhino sanctuary.

And of course, I am a bird lover's paradise. Twitchers from all around the world come to see the 450 different types of birds in Murchison Falls National Park. You will be amazed by the ground hornbills, secretary birds, black bellied bustards, open billed storks, weavers, and bee-eaters. One of the neatest birds is the shoebill stork that hangs out in the papyrus swamp area around the Delta. It has a huge beak and a very distinctive slow walk.

When you leave me, you will think three things: so green, so much nature, so friendly. When you drive by villages, children will run out of their houses to smile and wave to you.

5   A Drawer Full of Oatmeal

What country would you be visiting if someone gave you whisky and read you poetry on January 25th?

Here are some more hints.

1. I'm in Europe. I haven't been a country for 300 years, but many people still think of me as a country. I'm actually part of the United Kingdom.

2. When you think of me, think oatmeal. My people have eaten oatmeal for hundreds of years. In the days when men went out on the hill all day to look after sheep or cattle, they took a block of porridge with them. This was made by cooking oatmeal until it was very thick and then pouring it into a drawer and letting it harden.

3. My people call lakes lochs. Loch Ness is famous for a supposed monster that lives in the lake. People from all over the world have visited me to try to spot the Loch Ness monster.

4. I am the birthplace of one of the most famous poets on the planet: Robert Burns. Burns was born over 250 years ago, on January 25th, 1759, but the people of today still celebrate his birthday by having Burns' Night. For hours, they read his poetry and drink whisky.

Burns' poetry is so revered that famous writers have used lines from his poems for book titles. John Steinbeck called one of his books "Of Mice and Men", which came from a line in Burns' poem "To a Mouse". Burns wrote the poem "Auld Lang Syne", which people sing at New Year's (auld lang syne means times long past). An American astronaut, Nicholas Patrick, took a miniature book of Burns' poetry into orbit. American president Abraham Lincoln was a great admirer of Burns' poetry.

It's easy to see why Burns is so loved when you read the emotion in his poems. Here is his poem "Lines to an Old Sweetheart":

> Once fondly lov'd, and still remember'd dear,
> Sweet early object of my youthful vows,
> Accept this mark of friendship, warm, sincere,
> Friendship! 'tis all cold duty now allows.
> And when you read the simple artless rhymes,
> One friendly sigh for him, he asks no more,
> Who, distant, burns in flaming torrid climes,
> Or haply lies beneath th' Atlantic roar.

5. My people have names like Morag, Flora, Angus, and Robert. Their last names often start with Mac, like MacDougall, MacDuff, and MacAlister.

6. My country is named after a Celtic tribe that moved to my land from Ireland. They were called the Scots.

What country am I?

Answer: Scotland.

Points of Interest:

The United Kingdom (also called the United Kingdom of Great Britain and Northern Ireland) is a country made up of Scotland, England, Wales, and Northern Ireland.

My country is well-known for its Highlands and its Lowlands. There are even songs about them.

The largest land mammal in my country is the majestic red deer. It's truly an impressive animal and has wonderful large antlers.

6   I Am Not Russia!

What country would you be visiting if you saw a town deserted due to a nuclear reactor explosion?

Here are some more hints.

1. I am not Russia! Yes, Russia and I share a border, and yes, Russians have conquered me more than once, but my Slavic people and those of Russia have lived apart for so long that our cultures and our languages are different.

Okay, so maybe some Russian words are similar to my people's words, but we're still different! Anyhow, I've been independent from Russia since 1991. So you see, I'm not Russia!

2. The name for grandmother in my country is babushka. This name is also used for all elderly women. You'll see many babushki roaming around my cities, selling roasted sunflower seeds, flowers, or herbs, carrying large bundles, sweeping streets, or carrying pickaxes, shovels, or large buckets at a construction site.

These grannies have had tough lives, and they must work to live. Like most grannies, they love to feed their families and their guests. "Eat! Eat!" they cry. "You must eat to live!" My people have great respect for their babushki.

3. The town of Chernobyl is found in me. It's the site of the world's worst nuclear accident.

One day in 1986, two explosions blew apart reactor number 4 at the Chernobyl nuclear power station. Tons of radioactive particles were thrown one mile into the air.

Millions of people were exposed to the radiation; thousands were evacuated; people, animals, and plants died; women lost their babies or gave birth to babies with defects; children got thyroid cancer; and many people are still sick.

These days, Chernobyl is a ghost town; and for those brave enough, it's also a tourist attraction.

If you visit Chernobyl, you'll have to wear special clothing and you'll be checked for radiation during the tour. At the accident site, you'll be shown reactor number 4, which is now covered by a concrete building. This concrete building supposedly stops the 180 tons of radioactive material trapped inside the nuclear power plant from harming anyone.

4. If you visit me during the winter, you might see naked people running in the snow and jumping through holes in an ice-covered river for a swim. These people are called walruses. They practice an old form of Slavic yoga. They believe that bathing outdoors in the winter strengthens the immune system. But even the toughest walrus can't stand the cold water for more than 1 or 2 minutes. Despite the cold, all walruses get out of the water with a smile.

5. My people have names like Leonid Kravchuk, Tatiana Shevchenko, and Ivan Romanovych.

6. Most of my people speak Ukrainian. This is a big hint about my name.

What country am I?

Answer: Ukraine.

Points of Interest:

My people like their country to be called Ukraine, not THE Ukraine.

NB: In 2014, immediately after Russia hosted the winter Olympics, the President of Russia, Vladimir Putin, signed a piece of paper stating that Russia was annexing Ukraine. The world was shocked, and many countries made sanctions against Russia.

7 Fish Skin Jackets?

What country would you be in if you were having a business meeting in a sauna?

Here are some more hints.

1. I'm in northern Europe.

2. I'm the birthplace of the sauna. Many people have a sauna in their home and in their cottage. If you come to my country to do a business deal, don't be surprised if the company boss tells you that the meeting will take place in the company sauna.

Here's a lesson in sauna procedure: sit in a small room and sweat it out by pouring water over heated rocks. Do this until you feel faint. Then cool down in a cold shower; or if you're really brave, roll around in the snow or jump in an icy lake. I know it sounds painful, but it's actually very refreshing.

3. My winters are very cold. That's because I'm as far north as Iceland, Alaska, and Siberia. One third of my land is above the Arctic Circle, where there is continuous daylight for several weeks in summer and continuous darkness for several weeks in winter. It's like having one really long day, and one really long night. Some people find my long, dark winters very depressing. Maybe that's why my people are the biggest coffee drinkers in the world.

4. Mosquitoes are so bad in my country that my people hold a World Mosquito-Killing Championship each summer. The prize goes to the person who kills the most mosquitoes in a given amount of time using only the hands. One record was for 21 mosquitoes killed in five minutes. But be warned: my people are very good because they get so much practice.

5. My people have names like Eeva-Liisa Manner, Lasse Hallstrom, and Paavo Saarinen.

6. The name of my country means "land of the Finns". Finn comes from the Germanic word finna, which means fish scale. In early times, Finns wore clothes made of many different kinds of skins, including fish skins. Maybe that's how they got their name.

What country am I?

Answer: Finland.

Point of Interest:

If you visit me, you can go on a snow safari in Lapland province in the north. It lies mostly above the Arctic Circle and has snow ten months of the year. Lapland is huge and flat, and some areas have hardly any people. The Sami have lived in Lapland for thousands of years, and some still herd reindeer.

For fun, you can hire a guide to take you on a reindeer sled or a dog sled. Then you can set out across one of the many frozen lakes and take a journey into nowhere. But don't be surprised if your guide's cell phone rings. My people are cell phone crazy! This is hardly surprising since Nokia, which makes cell phones, has its roots in my country.

8 You Can Thank Me for Your French Fries

What country would you be in if you saw sloths hanging from trees?

Here are some more hints.

1. I'm in South America. Many of my people speak Spanish because Spain ruled me for almost 300 years.

2. If you visit me, you will see Native Peoples whose ancestors were part of the great Inca Empire.

3. Visit me and go on one of life's last great adventures: a trek through the Amazon jungle. Boat down the Amazon River, and you'll see large parrots, sloths hanging from trees, howler monkeys, dolphins, and piranhas. On shore, visit with tribesmen. But don't go off the beaten path: you might get lost or bitten by a snake.

4. For fun, visit the sultry port city of Iquitos, which has 370,000 people. Go to the market and buy a love potion, canoe through floating suburbs that have houses built on rafts, and enjoy the party-till-dawn nightlife. Iquitos is a major city with everything the international traveler could want, from Internet cafes to discotheques. But getting to Iquitos is a bit tricky because it has no roads to the outside world. You have to get to Iquitos by boat or by plane.

5. If you decide to hike in my Andes mountains, take it easy. For the first couple of days, you may get altitude sickness due to a lack of oxygen, and this is no laughing matter: altitude sickness makes you feel dizzy, nauseated, and headachy. If you exert yourself too much, every breath can become a labored gasp. Here's some advice: if you sleep in a motel high in the mountains, don't close your bedroom windows before you go to sleep. You may use up all the oxygen in the room!

6. If you visit my capital city, Lima, you may be overwhelmed: it's crowded with 8 million people, has a lot of smog, and one-third of its people live in shantytowns, where poor people build houses from cardboard, reed mats, scrap metal, and lumber. Lima also has glitzy, upscale suburbs like Miraflores, which are home to Lima's rich and famous. So, while some people scavenge for a living, others drive Mercedes cars filled with designer shopping bags.

7. If you scramble the letters of my name, you can spell "pure".

What country am I?

Answer: Peru.

Points of Interest:

Drug trafficking is a huge problem in my country. For hundreds of years, my people used the coca plant (not to be confused with the cocoa plant) for teas, medicine, and spiritual purposes. In the mid-1800s, some Spanish people living in my country started growing the coca plant for its cocaine. A lot of my farmland is now being used to grow coca plants. Cocaine drug-running has become a billion dollar industry. It causes a lot of crime, terrorism, and government corruption, so Peru is not so pure.

I'm the birthplace of the potato, so you can thank me for your French fries. When the Spaniards conquered my people, they stole their gold and silver, but the biggest prize they took back to Europe was the potato, although they didn't know it at the time. For 200 years, Europeans refused to eat potatoes. Because potatoes are bumpy and odd-looking, Europeans thought eating potatoes could cause odd and bumpy-looking skin conditions, like leprosy and warts. Today, people love potatoes. World trade in potatoes amounts to 100 billion dollars per year.

9 The Smallest Country in the World

What country would you be visiting if you were in the smallest country in the world?

Here are some more hints.

1. I'm on the continent of Europe.

2. I'm the size of a golf course. You can walk across me in 15 minutes.

3. I'm the most popular tourist destination in the world, even though I don't have beaches or resorts. Thousands of tourists visit me each day to see my famous museums and my famous church, St. Peter's Basilica.

4. If you visit me, you'll feel like you've stepped back in time. My security people wear fancy uniforms designed hundreds of years ago. In the butcher shop, you might see a man in the uniform of Napoleon's army ordering lamb chops, and in the pharmacy you might see a man wearing the red tunic and high boots of the royal cavalry of Spain asking for antacids. On the streets you might see Swiss Guards in their bright blue, yellow, and red striped uniform. They carry halberds. These are tall weapons that can be used as both a spear and a battle axe.

5. Visit me, and you'll see lots of nuns, bishops, and priests running around and maybe a cardinal or two.

6. In the summer, you might see the Pope, my Head of State, taking off in a helicopter to go to his house in the hills. My hot summer weather is very tiring.

What country am I?

Answer: The Vatican City.

Points of Interest:

Vatican City is found in Rome, Italy. I'm home to a thousand people.

One of my popes, Pope John XXIII, was known for his sense of humor. When a visitor asked him how many people actually worked in Vatican City, he answered, "Oh, about half of them."

Another one of my popes, Pope Paul VI, was a very active Pope: the first ever to appear before the United Nations. Facing the representatives from 117 countries, all armed to the teeth against their neighbors, he argued passionately for peace. "The hour has struck for a halt," he told them. "If you wish to be brothers, let the arms fall from your hands. One cannot love while holding offensive arms, especially those terrible arms which modern science has given you. Long before they produce victims and ruins, they nourish bad feelings and create nightmares and distrust. No more war, never again war!" The entire assembly rose to its feet and applauded.

10 National Voodoo Day

What country would you be visiting if you saw a voodoo parade?

Here are some more hints.

1. I'm a country on the continent of Africa. French is my national language because France ruled me for 60 years.

2. In my country, there are many witches and sorcerers. That's because I'm home to voodoo, the most popular religion in my country. In the voodoo religion, every animal, plant, and thing, such as mountains, rocks, and lakes, has a spirit created by God. Strong spirits can bring good or bad luck. People can influence these spirits by saying prayers and making offerings in their honor.

To become a voodoo priest or priestess, men and women go to voodoo school. They live a simple life and learn chants, dances, and the secrets of voodoo that they can't tell to outsiders. On graduation, the students are told, "Be responsible to the land, the spirits, your ancestors, and your fellow priests," and they are given a handful of their native soil to remind them of this. Voodoo has good and bad magic. Good magic is made up of spells and charms that turn away evil. Bad magic hurts people. Sorcerers who practice evil magic are hated.

Visit me on January 10, National Voodoo Day, and you'll see colourful and noisy voodoo parades. The holiday was started by President Soglo, who said that voodoo spirits saved his life.

3. If you visit my sacred Voodoo Python Temple, ask to have a Royal Python draped over you. But be careful: pythons can pee on you.

4. I was home to the great Dahomey kingdom, which had women in powerful positions like judges, spies, and soldiers.

5. My people have names like Efosa (e-FO-sa), Ewean (A-win), and Itohan (E-to-han).

6. My largest city is Cotonou. It's on a bay called the Bight of Benin. This is a big hint about my name.

What country am I?

Answer: Benin.

Points of Interest:

If you come to my country, why not visit Grand Popo, a coastal town on the beach overlooking the Gulf of Guinea, which is part of the Atlantic Ocean.

As you drive along the highway to Grand Popo, you will see huts with little white flags flying over them. This is where voodoo practitioners live and sell their services.

At the Grand Popo market, there are many voodoo artifacts to buy.

Here's a big word of warning: do not swim in the water at Grand Popo because there's a fierce riptide and people die there every year. It is much better to just relax on the beach and watch the local fisherman as they work on their nets.

* * * * *

Free Sample from "What Should I Do?" Series

Taken from The King's Poison Bread, which is 1 of 9 books from the "What Should I Do?" series.

<u>King Ou-ling: I'll Be a Laughing Stock</u>

What would you do if you were a king, and your people didn't want to wear a new kind of clothing?

The year is 307 BC. My name's Ou-ling. I'm the king of a state in China. My land is next to the Asian steppe, a flat grassland where many barbarian tribes live. These tribes often attack us.

At the moment, I'm in a meeting with one of my ministers. "We need to improve our army," I tell my minister. "Our barbarian enemies, the Hu, have had horse-soldiers for 100 years. Their horses are faster than our chariots. If we want to defeat the Hu, we'll have to train soldiers to ride horses."

My minister nods. "This is a good idea, Your Majesty, but how can we do this? Our people wear long robes tied at the waist with a belt. This makes it impossible for us to ride horses."

I shrug. "Then we'll have to start wearing pants and a short jacket like the Hu."

My minister is shocked. "But Your Highness, our people won't like it. They hate the Hu. If we start dressing like the Hu and riding horses like the Hu, our people will think we've become uncivilized."

I give him a determined look. "My mind is made up. I want you to call together my ministers."

My minister nods gravely and says, "Very well, Your Majesty."

On the day of the meeting, I announce my plans to have horse-soldiers who wear pants. Many of my ministers are shocked. One of them says, "But Your Majesty, to dress like a barbarian is the same as becoming a barbarian." Another minister says, "Your Majesty, our state is respected far and wide; but if we dress in pants, we'll all be laughing stocks."

I turn to Fei I, one of my ministers, and say, "What do you think?"

Fei I says, "Your Majesty, it is said that he who hesitates in his plans does not get the glory; he who hesitates in his actions, never achieves a great name. Therefore, My King, if you have decided to do good for your people, you'll have to ignore any criticism you get. Often, those who do the greatest good do not think the same way as the crowd. Therefore, My King, why do you hesitate?"

Two choices face me: I can continue with my plan to have horse-soldiers who will wear pants and a short jacket, or I can find another way to beat the Hu.

What should I do?

Answer:

I continued with my plan to have horse soldiers. Facing my ministers, I said, "I'll be the first to wear pants and a short jacket. Maybe I'll be a laughing stock, but I don't care. We have a lot to gain by having horse soldiers." In no time, my people got used to the new way of dressing; and when they saw how good the new army was, my idea was seen as a stroke of genius. Soon, cavalries became a necessary part of every army. Within 100 years, soldiers riding horses completely replaced chariots as the fast, striking arm of the army.

Point of Interest:

Would you be willing to dress in very different clothes than you do now if it was for the good of your country? For example, imagine there was an energy crisis in your country and scientists came up with a solution: they invented a purple pantsuit with embedded solar cells that could be worn by people during the day to capture the energy of the Sun, and at night the purple pantsuit could be hooked up to a household outlet to transfer the power to the city's energy grid. But in order for this solution to the energy crisis to work, everyone would have to wear the purple pantsuit every day during daylight hours. Would you agree to wear the purple pantsuit?

It's the journey, not the destination.

TITLES BY MC PAQUIN

Fiction Book

Fen Parker: Wormhole Chronicles
Reluctant Time Traveler

What Should I Do? Series

The Sphinx & the Pharaoh

Cleopatra's Carpet Trick

Michelangelo's Problem Apprentice

Saved by the Tail of an Ox

The King's Poison Bread

The Hand of Peace; The Hand of War

Lost, Starving, and Naked in the New World

The Real Robinson Crusoe

Lincoln in Love

What Country Am I? Series

Possums in the Attic

A Beauty Contest for Men

Look a Gorilla in the Eye

Very Short Picture History Books

Yay! A Short Picture History of Canada in 60 Minutes!

Yay! A Short Picture History of the USA in 60 Minutes!

Printed in Great Britain
by Amazon